Leap wants to study dinosaurs!

 Count the dinosaurs in each group.

 Draw a line between the groups with the same **number**.

Leap and his family are at the museum where they can learn about the dinosaurs from long ago. Dinosaur bones are put together to show how *big* the dinosaurs were.

Count the bones in each group. Write the number on the line. When you see this symbol **+**, that means that you should **add** the numbers together. Then, write the answer to show the total number of bones. The answer is also called the **sum**.

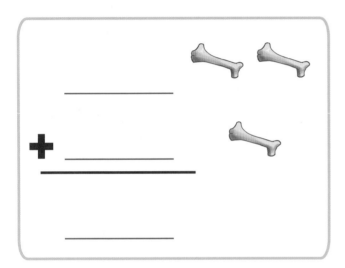

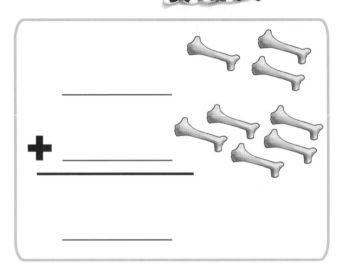

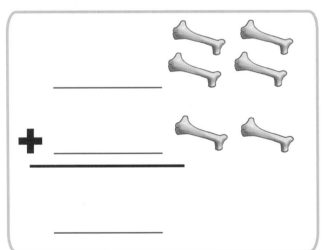

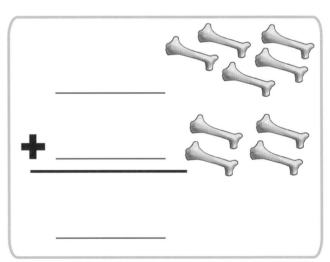

Get Moving!

Move and make sounds like a dinosaur! Walk on your toes.
Next, walk on all fours with your hands and feet on the ground.
Then run on two legs. Try moving slow and then fast.
What else do dinosaurs do?

Dad says that dinosaur bones are very old.
They are called fossils.

$$8$$
$$+4$$
_____

$$-----$$

Add. Write the sum.

$$7$$
$$+1$$
_____

$$9$$
$$+1$$
_____

$$5$$
$$+1$$
_____

$$6$$
$$+1$$
_____

$$9$$
$$+2$$
_____

$$8$$
$$+2$$
_____

$$6$$
$$+2$$
_____

$$7$$
$$+2$$
_____

$$9$$
$$+3$$
_____

$$7$$
$$+3$$
_____

$$8$$
$$+3$$
_____

$$5$$
$$+3$$
_____

Leap looks at the fossils of many different dinosaurs.

 Read each problem. Write the correct numbers on the lines at the right. Then, **add** the numbers together and write the **sum**.

Leap finds **4**  fossils.

Lily finds **3** more fossils.

How many fossils did they find in all?

$$4$$
$$+\ 3$$
_____

_____

Tad finds **8** fossils.

Leap finds **1** more fossil.

How many fossils did they find in all?

_____

$+$ _____

_____

Lily finds **6** fossils.

Tad finds **4** more fossils.

How many fossils did they find in all?

_____

$+$ _____

_____

Leap finds **9** fossils.

Tad and Lily find **2** more fossils.

 How many fossils did they find in all?

_____

$+$ _____

_____

Professor Quigley is at the museum, too. He helps Lily and Tad find more dinosaur fossils.

Read each problem. Write the correct numbers on the lines at the right. Then, **add** the numbers together and write the **sum**.

Professor Quigley shows Lily **7** fossils.

Lily finds **6** more fossils.

How many fossils did they find in all?

$$\begin{array}{r} 7 \\ + 6 \\ \hline \\ \hline \end{array}$$

Professor Quigley shows Tad **8** fossils.

Tad finds **3** more fossils.

How many fossils did they find in all?

$$\begin{array}{r} \rule{2cm}{0.4pt} \\ + \rule{2cm}{0.4pt} \\ \hline \\ \hline \end{array}$$

Professor Quigley shows Leap **9** fossils.

Leap finds **4** more fossils.

How many fossils did they find in all?

$$\begin{array}{r} \rule{2cm}{0.4pt} \\ + \rule{2cm}{0.4pt} \\ \hline \\ \hline \end{array}$$

Professor Quigley shows Tad and Lily **9** fossils.

Tad and Lily find **8** more fossils.

How many fossils did they find in all?

$$\begin{array}{r} \rule{2cm}{0.4pt} \\ + \rule{2cm}{0.4pt} \\ \hline \\ \hline \end{array}$$

Dinosaurs that ate plants were called herbivores or plant-eaters. This dinosaur saw **6** plants. He is going to take away **2** plants to eat. How many plants are left?

$$\begin{array}{r} 6 \\ -2 \\ \hline 4 \end{array}$$

Cross out and **subtract**. Write how many are left. When you see this symbol **–**, that means that you will take away or **subtract** one number from another.

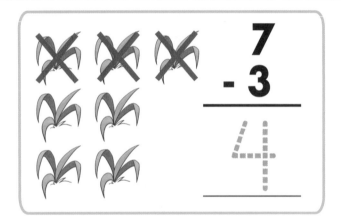

$$\begin{array}{r} 7 \\ -3 \\ \hline 4 \end{array}$$

$$\begin{array}{r} 5 \\ -3 \\ \hline \end{array}$$

$$\begin{array}{r} 4 \\ -4 \\ \hline \end{array}$$

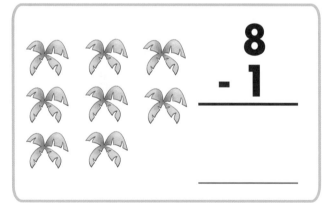

$$\begin{array}{r} 8 \\ -1 \\ \hline \end{array}$$

Get Moving!

With family or friends, play a game of musical chairs. Pretend that you are dinosaurs as you walk around the chairs. Roar your loudest roar! When the music stops, subtract one chair until only one person is left.

Other dinosaurs only ate insects, fish and different kinds of meat. They are called carnivores, or meat-eaters.

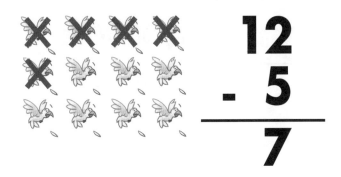

$$\begin{array}{r} 12 \\ -\ 5 \\ \hline 7 \end{array}$$

  Cross out and **subtract**. Write how many are left.

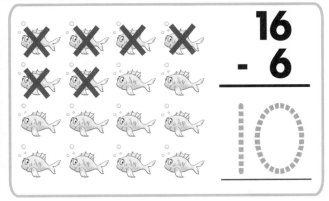

$$\begin{array}{r} 16 \\ -\ 6 \\ \hline 10 \end{array}$$

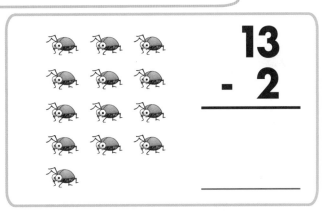

$$\begin{array}{r} 13 \\ -\ 2 \\ \hline \end{array}$$

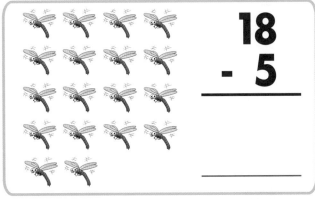

$$\begin{array}{r} 18 \\ -\ 5 \\ \hline \end{array}$$

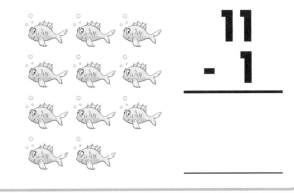

$$\begin{array}{r} 11 \\ -\ 1 \\ \hline \end{array}$$

$$\begin{array}{r} 17 \\ -\ 4 \\ \hline \end{array}$$

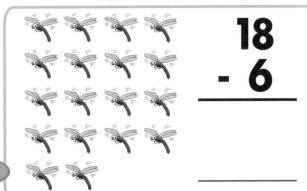

$$\begin{array}{r} 18 \\ -\ 6 \\ \hline \end{array}$$

The Oviraptor was an omnivore, who ate both meat and plants. Eggs were its favorite! It was called the "egg robber".

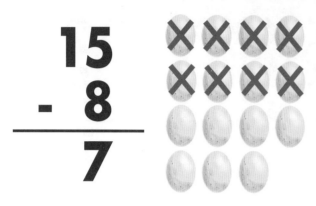

$$15 - 8 = 7$$

 Subtract. Write the answer.

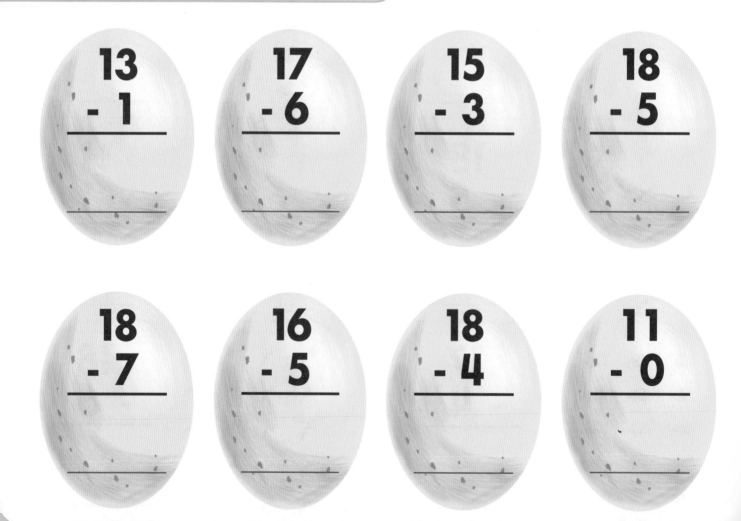

13 - 1

17 - 6

15 - 3

18 - 5

18 - 7

16 - 5

18 - 4

11 - 0

The museum gives away bookmarks of the many different kinds of dinosaurs.

 Read each problem. Write the correct number on the lines at the right. Then, **subtract** and write the answer.

Leap has **14** s.

He gives **3** s to Dad.

How many s does he have left?

$$14$$
$$- \quad 3$$
_____

_____

Tad has **18** s.

He gives **2** s to Dot.

How many s does he have left?

_____
− _____
_____

Lily has **15** s.

She gives **3** s to Professor Quigley.

How many s does she have left?

_____
− _____
_____

Mom has **17** s.

She gives **7** s to Grandpa.

How many s does she have left?

_____
− _____
_____

Professor Quigley knows all about dinosaur teeth. He says some dinosaurs had more than **900** teeth and others had none!

 Write the number that comes **before** the number shown.

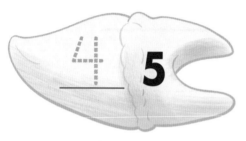 4 5

 15 16

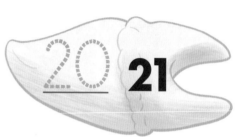 20 21

 _____ 29

 _____ 32

 _____ 37

 _____ 41

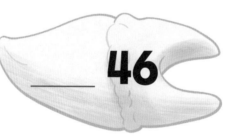 _____ 46

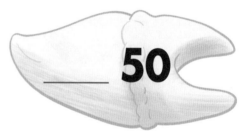 _____ 50

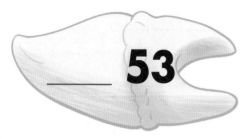 _____ 53

 _____ 57

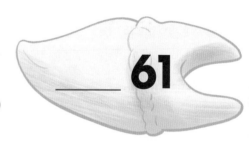 _____ 61

When a dinosaur lost a tooth, another one grew back in its place. The tooth grew back **after** the first one fell out.

 Write the number that comes **after** the number shown.

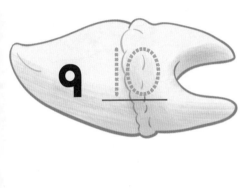 9 __10__

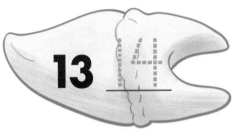 13 __14__

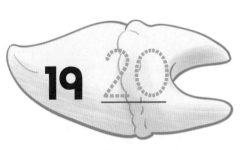 19 __20__

 24 ____

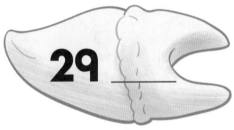 29 ____

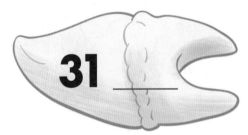 31 ____

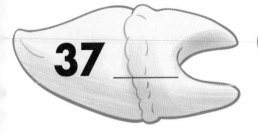 37 ____

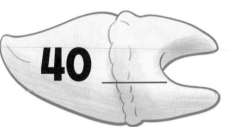 40 ____

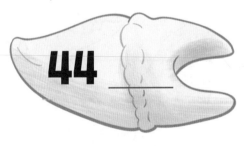 44 ____

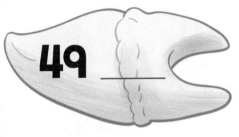 49 ____

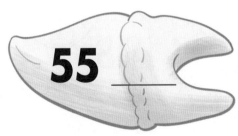 55 ____

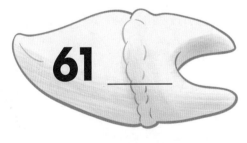 61 ____

Leap, Lily, and Tad learn about baby dinosaurs.

Draw a line to help the *baby dinosaur* find its mother. **Count** by **2's** to follow the path from **2** to **20**. **Counting** by **2's** is like skipping a number as you count.

START

2   4   6   8

2   4   6

2   2   4   8   10   12

4   6   8   10   14

6   7   12   14

6   8   16   15

8   10   18   20   FINISH

10   11

Dinosaurs drank water from rivers and streams.

  Count by **2's**.
Write the missing number.

2 4 ◯ 8 10 ◯ 14

2 4 6 ◯ 10 ◯ ◯ 16 18

2 4 6 ◯ 10 12 ◯ 16 18

2 4 ◯ ◯ 10 ◯ 14 16

2 4 6 8 10 ◯ ◯ ◯ 18

✾ Get Moving!

Play basketball using an empty bucket and a dry sponge. Every time you get the sponge in the bucket, you score two points. Record your score on paper. What else could you count by 2's?

Leap thinks the Stegosaurus looks cool.
He likes the spikes on its back.

Count by **5's** and draw a line to connect the dots from **5** to **100**. Color the picture.

65

90

40   70 85

45 60   95

35   75 80
15   50   55
20   30   100

10   25

5

• Skip counting by 5's • Fine motor skills

Professor Quigley explains the different time periods when dinosaurs lived.

Count by 5's.
Write the missing numbers.

Leap, Lily, and Tad are as hungry as dinosaurs!
Help them find their way to the snack bar.

Count by **10's** and draw a line to
follow the path from **10** to **100**.

• Skip counting by 10's • Fine motor skills

The snack bar is shaped like a giant dinosaur head.

1-2-3 **Count** by **10's**. Write the missing numbers.

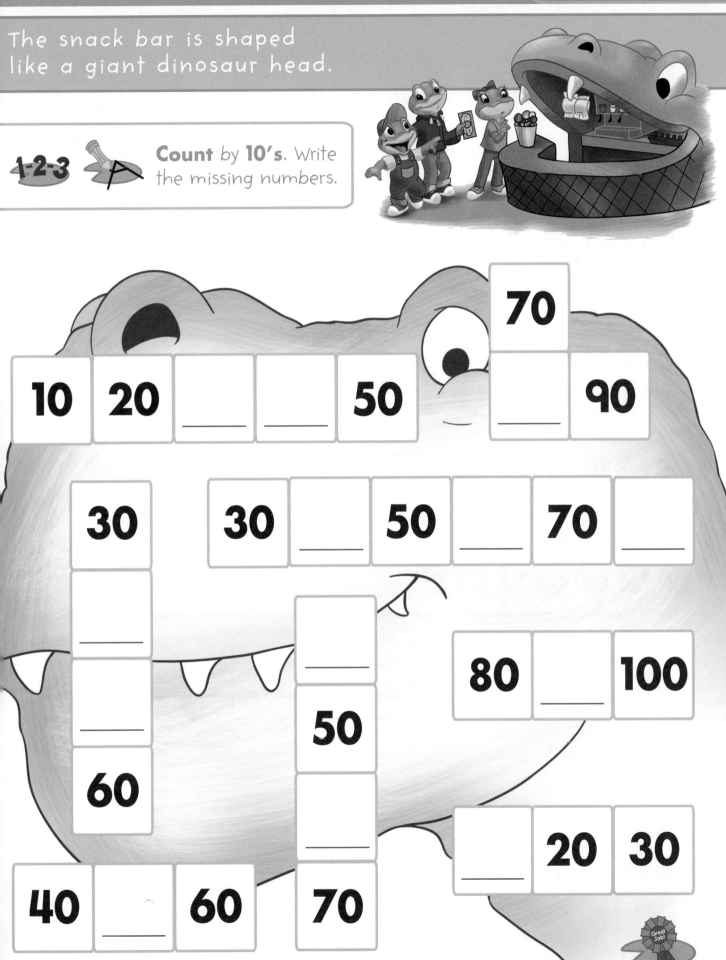

10 20 ___ ___ 50

70

___ 90

30

30 ___ 50 ___ 70 ___

___

___

60

80 ___ 100

50

___

40 ___ 60 70

___ 20 30

Tad found a penny. A **penny** is worth **one cent** or **1¢**. Counting pennies is like counting by **1's**.

 **Count** the money in each group. Draw a line to the correct amount.

6 ¢

9 ¢

13 ¢

14 ¢

 Draw the number of pennies needed to buy one dinosaur egg gumball.

5¢

Get Moving!

Go on a penny hunt! One person should hide some pennies around the room and then the other person has to find them. Count how many pennies you find! Look high and low!

Lily has a nickel. A **nickel** is worth **five cents** or **5¢**. One nickel is equal to five pennies. Counting nickels is like counting by **5's**.

 **Count** the money in each group. Draw a line to the correct amount.

 10 ¢

30 ¢

20 ¢

15 ¢

35¢

 Draw the number of nickels needed to buy one dinosaur chocolate bar.

Leap has a dime. A **dime** is worth **ten cents** or **10¢**. One dime is equal to two nickels. Counting dimes is like counting by 10's.

 **Count** the money in each group. Draw a line to the correct amount.

80 ¢

30 ¢

90 ¢

50 ¢

 Draw the number of dimes needed to buy one juice box.

Mom gives each of the children a quarter. A **quarter** is worth **twenty-five cents** or **25¢**. One quarter is equal to two dimes and one nickel.

 **Count** the money in each group. Draw a line to the correct amount.

                     25¢

                    50¢

                      75¢

 Draw the number of quarters needed to buy one bone-shaped pretzel.

Leap, Lily, and Tad bought dinosaur-shaped coin purses to hold their money.

Use the code to color the coins. **Count** the money in each group. Write the amount.

 = **red**   = **blue**   = yellow   = **green**

¢

_____

¢

_____

¢

_____

 Circle the one who has **more** money than the others.
Put an X on the one who has **less** money than the others.

Leap looks to find the year that his coins were made. Coins were made after dinosaurs disappeared.

Read each problem. Write the answer. Look at the coins in the magnifying glass to help you.

Leap has **3** pennies and **2** dimes.

How much money does he have in all? _____ ¢

Lily has **2** nickels and **3** dimes.

How much money does she have in all? _____ ¢

Tad has **2** pennies and **4** dimes.

How much money does he have in all? _____ ¢

Mom has **2** nickels and **1** quarter.

How much money does she have in all? _____ ¢

Lily always likes to know what time it is. The **little hand points to the hour** and the **big hand points to the minute**. When the little hand is on the **11** and the big hand is on the **12**, it is **11:00**.

Look at each clock.
Circle the correct **time**.

4:00   ⟨ 5:00 ⟩

8:00   9:00

1:00   2:00

3:00   4:00

10:00   11:00

7:00   8:00

9:00   10:00

6:00   7:00

12:00   2:00

When the big hand and the little hand are both on the **12**, it is **12:00**. At **12:00**, Leap and his family eat lunch at the museum.

  Look at each clock. Write the **time**.

10 : 00

.

.

.

.

.

.

.

.

Get Moving!

Watch the clock in your house. When the second hand that is moving gets to the 12, start jogging in place. See if you can jog until it reaches the 12 again - that's one minute. What else can you do for one minute?

When the little hand is just past the **1** and the big hand is on the **6**, it is **1:30**. At **1:30**, Professor Quigley likes to write in his journal.

Look at each journal. Circle the correct **time**.

1:30   **2:30**

6:30   **7:30**

3:30   **4:30**

9:30   **10:30**

3:30   **4:30**

8:30   **9:30**

11:30   **12:30**

7:30   **8:30**

5:30   **6:30**

When the little hand is just past the **3** and the big hand is on the **6**, it is **3:30**. At **3:30**, Tad takes a nap.

  Look at each clock. Write the **time**.

3:30
_____

•
•
_____

•
•
_____

•
•
_____

•
•
_____

•
•
_____

•
•
_____

•
•
_____

Archeologists use special tools to study dinosaurs. They use different clocks to keep time, too.

Draw a line to connect the clocks with the same **time**.

5:00

2:30

9:00

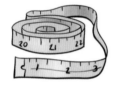

10:30

1:30

 What **time** do you wake up in the morning? _____

 What **time** do you go to bed at night? _____

Leap might want to be an archeologist when he grows up.

Help the archeologist find his way back to the lab. Draw a line through the path that shows **time** in the correct order.

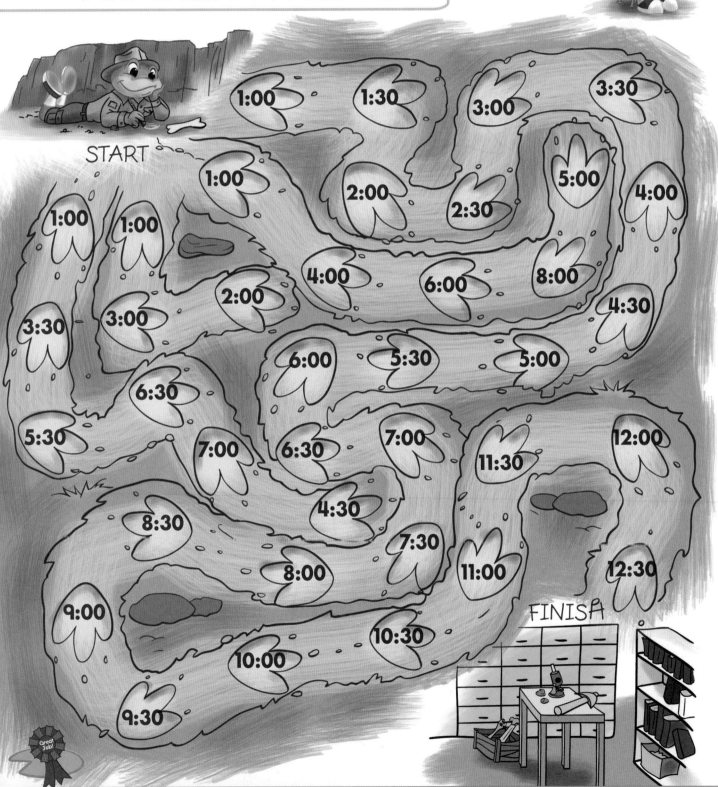

• Telling time to the hour and half hour

It's time to go home! It's **4:00**. Leap and his family have seen many different dinosaurs at the museum.

Add or **subtract**. Write the answers.
Then, color the picture according to the color code.

Answer is **1** = **green**

Answer is **2** = **purple**

Answer is **5** = **yellow**

Answer is **10** = **red**

Answer is **15** = **blue**

Answer is **20** = **orange**

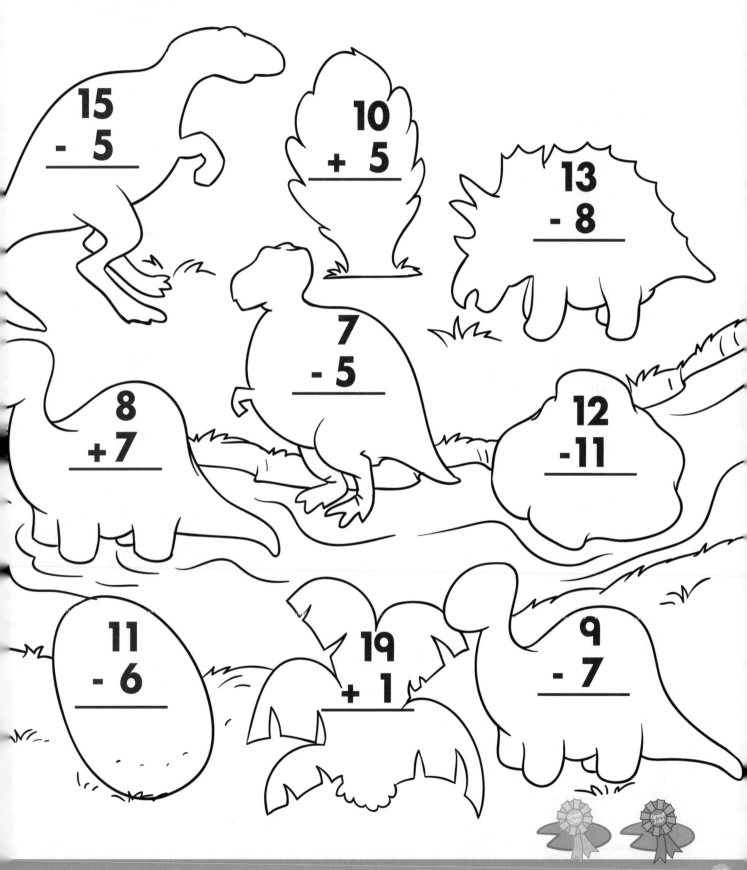

On the way home from the museum,
Leap talks about the fun they had.

Look at the pictures. Draw a line to match the **time** with the correct picture.

What is your favorite **time** of day?
Write the **time** on the clock.
Draw your favorite activity.

• Putting things in order • Telling time • Fine motor skills • Creativity